Search and Find

Bible Stories

CONCORDIA PUBLISHING HOUSE · SAINT LOUIS

Copyright © 2015 Concordia Publishing House

3558 S. Jefferson Ave., St. Louis, MO 63118-3968

1-800-325-3040 • www.cph.org

Scriptures are from the ESV Bible® (The Holy Bible, English Standard Version®), copyright © 2001 by Crossway Bibles, a publishing ministry of Good News Publishers. Used by permission. All rights reserved.

Illustrations by Michelle Dorenkamp-Repa / © CPH

Manufactured in Shenzhen, China/055760/330109

Table of Contents

1. Creation 4

2. Noah 6

3. Tower of Babel 8

4. Birth of Moses 10

5. Passover 12

6. Crossing the Red Sea 14

7. Water from the Rock 16

8. Rahab Believes 18

9. Hannah's Prayer 20

10. Elijah at the Brook Cherith 22

11. Elijah and the Widow of Zarephath 24

12. Elijah and the Prophets of Baal 26

13. Naaman Healed 28

14. Isaiah Sees the Lord 30

15. King Josiah 32

16. Jonah 34

17. The Birth of Jesus 36

18. John the Baptist 38

19. Wedding at Cana 40

20. Built on the Rock 42

21. Jesus Heals at Bethesda 44

22. Jesus Stills the Storm 46

23. Jesus and Nicodemus 48

24. Good Samaritan 50

25. Mary and Martha 52

26. Parable of the Ten Virgins 54

27. Triumphal Entry 56

28. The Widow's Mite 58

29. Jesus Is Anointed 60

30. Jesus Washes Disciples' Feet 62

31. Jesus in the Garden 64

32. Jesus Suffers and Dies 66

33. On the Road to Emmaus 68

34. Jesus Ascends to Heaven 70

35. God Sends the Holy Spirit 72

36. Philip and the Ethiopian 74

37. Peter's Escape from Prison 76

38. Lydia 78

39. Paul's Shipwreck 80

40. The River of Life 82

Family Faith Talks for all stories, pages 84–88

1
Creation

Genesis 1–2

In the beginning, God created the heavens and the earth. On each day of creation, God made a different part of the world around us.

After five days, God said, "Let the earth bring forth living creatures according to their kinds." And it was so. And God made the animals. And God saw that it was good.

Then God said, "Let Us make man in Our image, after Our likeness. Let them rule over the fish and the birds, and over the animals." So God created man in His own image, in the image of God He created him; male and female He created them. God saw everything that He had made, and it was very good. And there was evening and there was morning, the sixth day.

Thus the heavens and the earth were finished, and everything that filled them. On the seventh day, God finished His work, and rested. So God blessed the seventh day and made it holy.

Search and Find

1 sun

8 raspberries

4 clouds

2 water birds

3 stars

3 rocks

1 man

1 mouse

1 Bible

Jesus' face

1 owl

5 white flowers

1 binoculars

4 shrubs

10 apples

1 worm

1 fish

6 fireflies

2
Noah

Genesis 6:9–9:17

The Lord saw the wickedness of man was great in the earth and all that man thought about was doing evil. But Noah found favor in the eyes of the Lord, along with his three sons, Shem, Ham, and Japheth.

God said to Noah, "Make an ark. Behold I will bring a flood upon the earth to destroy all things." Noah did all God commanded.

The Lord shut Noah, his family, and the animals in the ark. Then fountains of the deep burst, and the windows of the heavens were opened and rain fell upon the earth forty days and forty nights. Only Noah and those with him were safe.

Later, God made a wind blow over the earth—the waters subsided. The ark came to rest on the mountains of Ararat. So Noah and his sons and his wife and his son's wives and every beast went out from the ark.

Noah built an altar to the Lord and offered burnt offerings. God told Noah and his sons, "Never again shall there be a flood to destroy the earth. I have set my bow in the clouds as a sign of the covenant that I make between Me and you."

Search and Find

 1 Bible

 5 flowers

 1 bird

 2 bears

 1 door

 Jesus' face

 4 windows

 11 rocks

 1 man with a coat

1 blue jar

1 green scarf

2 dogs

1 rainbow

7 shells

1 giraffe

1 man with a gray beard

3 clouds

5 trees

3
Tower of Babel

Genesis 9:18–19; 11:1–9

After the flood, all the people on earth were descendants of Noah's three sons. Everyone on earth spoke the same language.

The people said, "Let's build a tower with its top in the heavens. Then we can make a name for ourselves. We can stay here and not be scattered across the whole earth."

God saw what they were doing and said, "Look, the people are staying together in one place and speak only one language. It seems nothing will stop them from doing whatever they want. Let Us go down and confuse their language so they will not be able to understand one another."

So the Lord confused their languages and scattered the people all over the earth. They had to stop building the tower. The city is called Babel because the Lord confused the language of the earth. From there, the Lord scattered the people all over the earth.

 Search and Find

4 flowers

Jesus' face

1 worker
with a
blue shirt

4 ladders

12 stone blocks

8 birds

1
red-haired worker

3 donkeys

6 windows

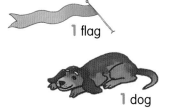
1 flag

1 dog

1 Bible

HOLY BIBLE

1 tar pot

5 wheelbarrows

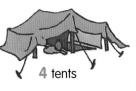
4 tents

5 palm trees

4
Birth of Moses
Exodus 1:8–2:1

The sons of Israel who came to Egypt had many children. They grew strong. Then Pharaoh told his people, "Every son that is born to the Hebrews you shall throw into the Nile River."

A Levite woman hid her newborn son for three months. When she could hide him no longer, she made a basket, put the child in it, and put the basket among the reeds by the riverbank.

The daughter of Pharaoh came down to bathe at the river. Pharaoh's daughter saw the basket among the reeds. When she opened it, she saw the child. Pharaoh's daughter took pity on him.

And Pharaoh's daughter said to the mother, "Take this child away. Nurse him for me. I will give you wages." So the woman took the child. And when the child grew up, she brought him to Pharaoh's daughter. Then he became her son. She named him Moses.

Search and Find

Jesus' face

1 cat

1 basket

Miriam

10 cattails

1 cat dish

2 turtles

3 fish

6 water lilies

1 blue scarf

1 dragonfly

5 frogs

7 palm trees

1 Bible

1 necklace

5
Passover

Exodus 12:1–28; 13:14

The Lord promised to send one more plague upon Pharaoh and Egypt. About midnight, every firstborn in the land of Egypt would die.

The Lord said to Moses and Aaron, "Kill some lambs at twilight. Then take some of the blood and put it on the doorposts of the houses. Eat the meat that night, roasted on the fire. You shall eat it with your belt on, your sandals on your feet, and your staff in your hand. It is the Lord's Passover. For I will pass through the land of Egypt that night. I will strike all the firstborn in the land of Egypt. I am the Lord. The blood shall be a sign for you on the houses where you are. And when I see the blood, I will pass over you."

At midnight, the Lord struck down all the firstborn in the land of Egypt. And there was a great cry in Egypt, for there was not a house where someone was not dead.

Then Pharaoh told Moses and Aaron, "Up! Go out from among my people. Go, serve the Lord, as you have said. Be gone, and bless me also!"

Search and Find

1 Bible

2 walking sticks

1 angel

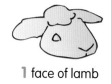
1 face of lamb

1 cat

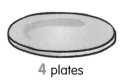
4 plates

1 trail sign

4 goblets

8 stars

Jesus' face

2 birds

4 glasses

11 sandals

1 red belt

3 loaves
of flat bread

6
Crossing the Red Sea

Exodus 14

When Pharaoh, the king of Egypt, was told that the people had fled, he said, "What have we done, that we let Israel go?" Pharaoh—along with all his chariots, horsemen, and the army—pursued the people of Israel. The army overtook the people of Israel as they were camped along the sea.

When Pharaoh drew near, the people of Israel were afraid. They cried out to the Lord. Moses said, "Fear not. Stand firm. The Lord will fight for you."

The Lord said to Moses, "Lift up your staff, and stretch out your hand over the sea and divide it. Then the people may go through the sea on dry ground." When Moses stretched out his hand, the Lord drove back the sea with a strong wind. God made the sea dry land. The people of Israel walked through the middle of the sea on dry ground. When the Egyptian army tried to follow them, the pillar of fire and cloud threw the Egyptian forces into a panic.

As the Egyptian army attempted to flee, Moses stretched out his hands once again. The waters returned and covered the chariots and horsemen. Not one of Pharaoh's army remained. Thus the Lord saved Israel.

Search and Find

2 sheep

3 children

1 walking stick

1 road map

1 Bible

2 chariots

3 horses

1 red coat

5 sandals

6 birds

2 waves

1 lifesaving ring

9 fish

2 jugs

Jesus' face

4 spears

Man with a brown beard

2 green headbands

3 bags

1 soldier helmet

7
Water from the Rock

Exodus 17:1–7

The people of Israel came into the wilderness. There was no water for the people, and they quarreled with Moses, saying, "Why have you brought us out of Egypt to kill us and our children and our livestock with thirst?" for there was no water in that place.

Moses called to the Lord, "What shall I do? The people are ready to stone me!" The Lord replied, "Take the staff with which you struck the Nile and go to the rock at Horeb. Strike the rock, and water will come forth for the people and their livestock."

So Moses went and struck the rock, and water came out abundantly. The people drank and provided water for their cattle, using the water from the rock.

Search and Find

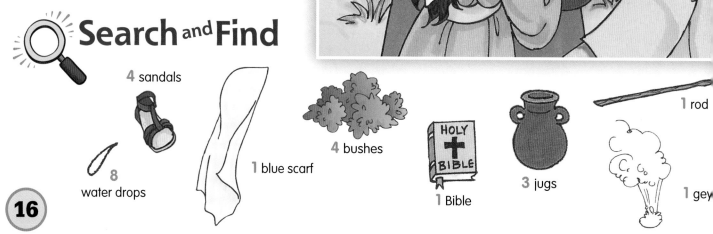

4 sandals

8 water drops

1 blue scarf

4 bushes

1 Bible

3 jugs

1 rod

1 geyser

1 yellow sash

6 rocks

1 sun

1 surprised look

1 man with
a red beard

1 striped coat

2 lizards

1 snake

Jesus' face

8
Rahab Believes
Joshua 2

Joshua sent two men as spies. In Jericho, they came into the house of Rahab. And the king of Jericho was told, "Behold, men of Israel have come here tonight to search out the land."

Then the king sent a message to Rahab. He said, "Bring out the men who have come to you. They have come to search out all the land."

But Rahab took the men up to the roof to hide them. She said, "I know that the Lord has given you the land. The Lord is your God. He is God in the heavens and on the earth. Give me a sign that you will save my family and deliver our lives from death."

The men said to her, "If you do not tell on us, then when the Lord gives us the land, we will be kind to you." Then she let them down by a rope through a window. And she said, "Go into the hills! Hide for three days; then go on your way."

The men said, "When we come again, tie this scarlet cord in the window, and gather your family into your house."

Then she sent them away.

Search and Find

2 trees

10 bolts
4 bushes
2 spies

1 moon
6 nails
5 swords
1 snake
7 stars

Rahab

3
bundles of flax

1 sun

2 rabbits

1 Bible

Jesus' face

10 stones

1 red cord

9
Hannah's Prayer

1 Samuel 1:1–2:21

Now Eli the priest was sitting on the seat beside the doorpost of the temple of the Lord. Hannah prayed to the Lord and wept bitterly. She vowed a vow and said, "O Lord of hosts, if You will give to Your servant a son, then I will give him to the Lord all the days of his life."

Eli answered, "Go in peace. The God of Israel grant your prayer."

The Lord remembered Hannah, and she gave birth to a son. She called his name Samuel, for she said, "I have asked for him from the Lord."

When Hannah had weaned Samuel, she brought Him to the house of the Lord. They brought the child to Eli. Hannah said, "I am the woman who was standing here, praying to the Lord. The Lord has granted me my prayer. Therefore, as long as he lives, this child is lent to the Lord."

Search and Find

2 cats

3 flowers

1 blue belt

1 green sash

2 spiders

2 stars

1 head scarf

Jesus' face

1 Bible

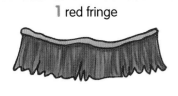
1 red fringe

1 tree

5 rectangles

10 tassels

6 carvings

10
Elijah at the Brook Cherith

1 Kings 17:1–6

King Ahab was more evil than all the kings that came before him. He worshiped a false god named Baal.

The prophet Elijah went to Ahab. Elijah warned the king, "God says there will be no rain—not even dew—for years, except by My word."

Then the Lord told Elijah, "Hide yourself by the brook Cherith. You shall drink from the brook, and I have commanded the ravens to feed you there." So Elijah did according to the word of the Lord. And the ravens brought Elijah bread and meat in the morning and in the evening, and he drank from the brook. After a while, the brook dried up, because there was no rain.

Then the word of the Lord came to Elijah, "Go to Zarephath. I have commanded a widow there to feed you."

Search and Find

4 lily pads

3 frogs

1 red coat

1 sun

3 clouds

Jesus' face

4 pieces of brea[d]

1 Bible

Water Cycle

3 bushes

6 rocks

7 tufts of grass

5 ravens

1 water cycle

1 rabbit

1 blue belt

11
Elijah and the Widow of Zarephath

1 Kings 17:8–24

Then God told Elijah, "Arise! Go to live in Zarephath. I told a widow there to feed you."

Elijah went to the city gate. He saw a widow gathering sticks. He called to her, "Bring me a little water. I would like a drink." As she was going for water, he also asked for bread.

She said, "I have only a handful of flour in a jar and a little oil in a jug. I am gathering sticks so I can make bread. We will eat it and die."

Elijah said, "Do not be afraid. Go and make bread. First, make me a little bread. Bring it to me. After that, make something for yourself and your son. God says, 'The jar of flour shall not run out. The jug of oil will not be empty, until the day I send rain to the earth.'"

She did as Elijah said. They ate for many days. The jar of flour did not run out. The jug of oil did not run out.

Search and Find

1 dog

2 vessels of water

1 Bible

1 caterpillar

Jesus' face

2 clouds

24

5 bushes

2 butterflies

2 hiking boots

2 ravens

3 loaves of bread

2 bundles of sticks

4
jars of oil

1 window

12
Elijah and the Prophets of Baal

1 Kings 18:20–46

Elijah and the 450 prophets of Baal gathered at Mount Carmel. Baal's prophets cut one bull in pieces and laid it on the wood, but put no fire to it. Elijah prepare the other bull and laid it on the wood and put no fire to it. Elijah said, "You call upon the name of your god. I will call upon the name of the Lord. The God who answers by fire, He is God."

The prophets of Baal called upon the name of Baal from morning until noon. But no one answered.

Elijah made a trench around the altar of the Lord. He had people fill four jars with water three times and pour the water on the offering and on the wood. The water ran around the altar and filled the trench.

Elijah prayed, "O Lord, God of Abraham, Isaac, and Israel, let it be known this day that You are God in Israel. Answer me, O Lord, so the people may know You, O Lord, are God." Then the fire of the Lord fell and consumed the burnt offering and the wood and the stones and the dust. It licked up the water that was in the trench.

When the people saw, they fell on their faces and said, "The Lord, He is God. The Lord, He is God."

 Search and Find

3 logs

2 goats

4 bushes

2 goats

4 bushes

1 rabbit

1 Bible

1 spider

3 clouds

1 gray beard

1 crown

6 burning sticks

1 praying hands

1 red coat

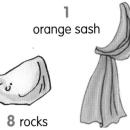
8 rocks

1 orange sash

Jesus' face

3 lizards

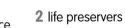
2 life preservers

13
Naaman Healed

2 Kings 5:1–14

Naaman was a leader in the army of the king of Syria, but he was a leper. A little servant girl told Naaman's wife, "My lord should go to Samaria! God's prophet there would cure his leprosy."

Naaman got ready to go. He took silver, gold, and ten changes of clothing. He took a letter from his king to the king of Israel that said, "I send Naaman my servant to you. Please cure his leprosy."

Naaman took his horses and chariots to Elisha's house. He stood at the door. Elisha sent out a servant with a message. The servant said, "Go and wash seven times in the Jordan River. Then your flesh shall heal. You shall be clean."

Naaman was angry. He went away. He said, "I thought Elisha would come. I thought he would call on the Lord his God. I thought he would wave his hand and cure me. The rivers of my country are better than all the waters of Israel!"

Naaman's servants said, "The prophet spoke great words. Do what he said, 'Wash, and be clean'!" Naaman went to the Jordan River. He dipped in it seven times. His skin was like the skin of a little child. He was clean.

Search and Find

3 fish

5 stars

4 palm trees

7 fingers

4 windows

2 jars

Elisha

1 eye wash sign

1 blue hat

1 snake

9 cattails

2 frogs

1 Bible

12 drops of water

6 shells

Jesus' face

8 flowers

14
Isaiah Sees the Lord

Isaiah 6:1–13

The prophet Isaiah wrote:

I saw the Lord sitting upon a throne. The train of His robe filled the temple. Above Him stood the seraphim. Each had six wings. With two wings, each covered his face. With two wings, each covered his feet. With two wings, each flew. And they called to one another and said:

"Holy, holy, holy is the Lord of hosts. The whole earth is full of His glory!"

The foundations of the thresholds shook at the voice of him who called. The house was filled with smoke. And I said: "Woe is me! For I am lost. For I am a man of unclean lips. I dwell in the midst of a people of unclean lips. For my eyes have seen the King, the Lord of hosts!"

Then one of the seraphim flew to me. He had in his hand a burning coal that he had taken with tongs from the altar. He touched my mouth and said: "Behold, this has touched your lips. Your sin is taken away."

And I heard the voice of the Lord. He said, "Whom shall I send? Who will go for Us?"

Then I said, "Here am I! Send me."

Search and Find

2 columns

2 suns

3 seraphim

1 yellow head covering

1 blue sash

7 burning coals

8 pomegranates

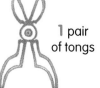
1 pair of tongs

1 Bible

Jesus' face

5 diamonds

4 flowers

18 wings

15
King Josiah

2 Kings 22:1–20

King Josiah was eight years old when he began to reign over Judah. When he was older, he sent Shaphan the secretary to the house of the Lord. Then Hilkiah, the high priest, spoke to Shaphan. He said, "I have found the Book of the Law in the house of the Lord."

When King Josiah heard the words of the Book of the Law, he tore his clothes in mourning. He said, "Go! Ask the Lord about the words of this book that has been found. For great is the wrath of the Lord. Our fathers have not obeyed the words of this book."

So Hilkiah the priest and Shaphan went to Huldah the prophetess.

Huldah said to them: "Thus says the Lord, the God of Israel: 'Behold, I will bring disaster upon this place. For they have forsaken Me. They have made offerings to other gods. But say to the king, Thus says the Lord, the God of Israel: Your heart was penitent. You humbled yourself before the Lord. So your eyes shall not see all the disaster that I will bring upon this place.'"

Search and Find

7 rocks

2 brushes

1 spider

7 boards

1 Bible

1 blue shirt

3 butterflies

1 crown

1 lizard

1 scroll

3 saws

4 hammers

2 suns

Jesus' face

1 man with red hair

6 moneybags

16
Jonah

Jonah 1–3

The word of the Lord came to Jonah. He said, "Arise, go to Nineveh. Call out against it. For their evil has come up before Me."

But Jonah rose to flee from the Lord. He found a ship. He went on board to go away from the LORD. But the Lord sent a great wind upon the sea. In fear, the sailors threw Jonah overboard.

And the Lord sent a great fish to swallow up Jonah. And Jonah was in the belly of the fish three days and three nights.

Then Jonah prayed to the Lord his God from the belly of the fish. And the Lord spoke to the fish. It vomited Jonah out upon the dry land.

Then the Lord said to Jonah again, "Arise, go to Nineveh. Call out against it the message that I tell you."

So Jonah went to Nineveh. He called out, "Yet forty days, and Nineveh shall be overthrown!" And the people of Nineveh believed God.

God saw that the people of Nineveh turned from their evil way. God relented of the disaster that He had said He would do to them. He did not do it.

Search and Find

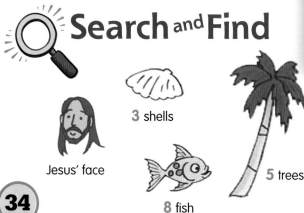

Jesus' face

3 shells

8 fish

5 trees

1 chest

1 sign

4 windows

1 Bible

3 crosse

34

2 sailors

4 clams

1 green sash

1 octopus

8 air bubbles

1 sunken ship

1 flag

17
The Birth of Jesus

Luke 2

The Roman ruler told all the people to register for a census. All went to be registered, each to his own town. Joseph also went to Bethlehem. He took Mary.

While there, the time came for her to give birth. She gave birth to her first child, a Son. She wrapped Him in cloths. She placed Him in a manger, for there was no room for them in the inn.

Not far away were shepherds out in the field, watching over their flock by night. The glory of the Lord shone around them. They were filled with fear.

An angel said, "Fear not. For behold! I bring you good news of a great joy for all people. To you is born this day a Savior. He is Christ the Lord. You will find a baby wrapped in cloths and lying in a manger."

Suddenly, there were many angels praising God, "Glory to God in the highest, and peace on earth!"

Then the shepherds said, "Let us go and see this thing."

They went quickly and found Mary and Joseph and the baby in a manger. When they saw it, they told others about the child.

Search and Find

Jesus' face

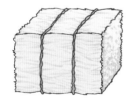

3 bales of straw

3 shepherd staffs

2 birds

2 sleeping bags

1 Bible

4 sheep

1 donkey face

2 lanterns

1 bucket

1 hammer

1 mouse

6 stars

2 angels

18
John the Baptist

Luke 3:1–20; John 1:19–34

Now John wore a garment of camel's hair and a leather belt around his waist. His food was locusts and wild honey. Jerusalem and all Judea and all the region about the Jordan were going out to him. They were baptized by John in the river Jordan, confessing their sins.

John said, "I baptize you with water for repentance, but He who is coming after me is mightier than I. I am not worthy to carry His sandals. He will baptize you with the Holy Spirit and fire."

Then Jesus came from Galilee to the Jordan to John, to be baptized by him.

John would have prevented Jesus. John said, "I need to be baptized by You, and do You come to me?"

Jesus answered, "Let it be so, for thus it is fitting for us to fulfill all righteousness." Then John consented.

When Jesus was baptized, immediately He went up from the water. Behold, the heavens were opened to Him. He saw the Spirit of God descending like a dove and coming to rest on Him. Behold, a voice from heaven said, "This is My beloved Son, with whom I am well pleased."

 Search and Find

 1 bee hive

 3 clouds

 10 rocks

1 brown belt

 LAMB OF GOD

 1 green hat

1 Bible

 1 soldier helm

LAMB OF GOD

HOLY BIBLE

5 bees

Jesus' face

2 lambs

2 turtles

1 flag

4 washcloths

8 flowers

6 bushes

1 man with black hair

1 yellow coat

19
Wedding at Cana

John 2:1–11

There was a wedding at Cana in Galilee. The mother of Jesus was there. Jesus also was invited to the wedding with His disciples.

When the wine ran out, the mother of Jesus said to Him, "They have no wine."

Now there were six stone water jars there for the Jewish rites of purification, each holding twenty or thirty gallons. Jesus said to the servants, "Fill the jars with water." They filled them up to the brim. Then Jesus said, "Now draw some out and take it to the master of the feast."

When the master of the feast tasted the water now become wine, and did not know where it came from, he called to the bridegroom. He said to him, "Everyone serves the good wine first, and when people have drunk freely, then they serve the poor wine. But you have kept the good wine until now."

This, the first of His signs, Jesus did at Cana in Galilee, and manifested His glory. And His disciples believed in Him.

Search and Find

1 candle

2 butterflies

4 flowers

2 bowls

1 Bible

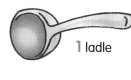
1 ladle

5 gifts

6 water jugs

5 goblets

1 flower wreath

Wine

6 stars

7 oranges

Jesus' face

1 man with surprised look

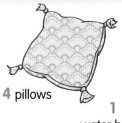
4 pillows

1 water bottle

20
Built on the Rock

Matthew 7:24–27;
Luke 6:47–49

Jesus was on the hillside teaching the people. He had been teaching for quite a while. Near the end of His sermon, Jesus told the people a story about two builders:

"Everyone then who hears these words of Mine and does them will be like a wise man who built his house on the rock. And the rain fell, and the floods came, and the winds blew and beat on that house, but it did not fall, because it had been founded on the rock. And everyone who hears these words of Mine and does not do them will be like a foolish man who built his house on the sand. And the rain fell, and the floods came, and the winds blew and beat against that house, and it fell, and great was the fall of it."

Search and Find

3 fish

5 boards

4 crabs

3 sand pails

10 raindr

1 sun

1 boat

2 sand shovels

7 trees

1 Bible

Jesus' face

1 rock wall

6 shells

3 windows

8 stones

4 lightning bolts

21
Jesus Heals at Bethesda

John 5:1–15

In Jerusalem, by the Sheep Gate, is a pool called Bethesda. A man was there who had been an invalid for thirty-eight years. When Jesus saw him lying there, He knew he had been there a long time. Jesus said to him, "Do you want to be healed?"

The sick man answered Him, "Sir, I have no one to put me into the pool when the water is stirred up, and while I am going, another steps down before me."

Jesus said to him, "Get up, take up your bed, and walk." At once, the man was healed, and he took up his bed and walked.

Search and Find

3 steps

4 crutches

1 rat

1 red head covering

3 canes

2 birds

4 bandages

1 Bible

1 blind man   6 clouds   Jesus' face   1 bandaged leg   6 mats   9 bubbles   1 black beard

22
Jesus Stills the Storm

Luke 8:22–25

One evening after Jesus had done a lot of teaching, He said, "Let us go across to the other side." And leaving the crowd, the disciples took Him with them in the boat.

A great windstorm arose. The waves came into the boat. They were so high that the boat was filling with water. Jesus was in the back of the boat, called the stern. He was asleep on the cushion.

The disciples woke Jesus. They said, "Teacher, do You not care? We are perishing!"

He awoke and rebuked the wind. He said to the sea, "Peace! Be still!" The wind stopped. There was a great calm.

Then Jesus said to them, "Why are you so afraid? Have you still no faith?"

The twelve disciples were filled with great fear. They said to one another, "Who then is this? Even the wind and sea obey Him!"

 Search and Find

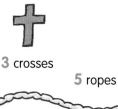

3 crosses

5 ropes

1 brown robe

3 accordion fans

Jesus' face

1 rain poncho

5 praying hands

6 small fish

2 big fish

2 oars

1 blue robe

1 Bible

23
Jesus and Nicodemus

John 3:1–16

There was a man named Nicodemus, a ruler of the Jews, who came to Jesus by night. He said to Jesus, "Rabbi, we know that You are a teacher come from God. No one can do these signs that You do unless God is with him."

Jesus said, "Truly, truly, I say to you, unless one is born again, he cannot see the kingdom of God."

Nicodemus said, "How can a man be born when he is old?"

Jesus said, "Truly, truly, I say to you, unless one is born of water and the Spirit, he cannot enter the kingdom of God. Do not marvel that I said to you, 'You must be born again.'"

Nicodemus said, "How can these things be?"

Jesus said, "Are you the teacher of Israel? You do not know these things? Truly, truly, I say to you, I have told you about things on earth. Remember how Moses lifted up the serpent in the wilderness? So must the Son of Man be lifted up. Whoever believes in Him may have eternal life."

Search and Find

2 cats

4 water jugs

Jesus' face

2 crescent moons

5 grape clusters

1 windsock

3 flashlights

5 flowers

6 crosses

1 Bible

7 shells

3 doves

1 moon

24
Good Samaritan

Luke 10:25–37

A lawyer said, "Teacher, how do I inherit eternal life?"

Jesus replied, "What is written in the Law"

He answered, "You shall love the Lord your God with all your heart and with all your soul and with all your strength and with all your mind, and your neighbor as yourself."

Jesus said, "You answered correctly; do this, and you will live."

Wanting to justify himself, he said, "Who is my neighbor?"

Jesus replied, "A man was going from Jerusalem to Jericho, and fell among robbers, who stripped him and beat him, leaving him half dead. Now a priest was going down the road. When he saw the man, he passed by on the other side. So likewise a Levite, when he saw him, passed by on the other side. But a Samaritan had compassion, went to him, and bound up his wounds. Then he set him on his own animal and brought him to an inn and took care of him. The next day, he took out two denarii and gave them to the innkeeper, saying, 'Take care of him, I will repay you when I come back.' Which proved to be a neighbor to the man?"

He said, "The one who showed mercy."

Jesus said, "Go, and do likewise."

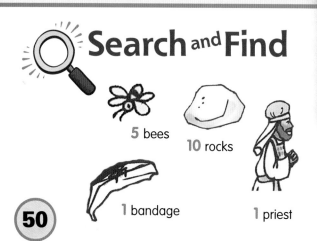

Search and Find

5 bees

10 rocks

1 bandage

1 priest

 9 flowers

 1 Bible

 1 scorpion

 1 man with black

1 blue hat

1 bottle

3 robbers

4 bushes

Jesus' face

2 bunnies

5 windows

1 red coat

25
Mary and Martha

Luke 10:38–42

One day, as Jesus traveled, He came to a village where a woman named Martha invited Him to her home. She had a sister named Mary, who sat at Jesus' feet and listened to Him teach.

Martha was concerned about everything that needed to be done to serve everyone, so she said to Jesus, "Lord, don't you care that my sister has left me to do all of the work by myself? Tell her to help me."

"Martha, Martha," Jesus answered her, "you are worried and upset about so many things, but you need only one thing, and Mary has chosen that good thing. It will not be taken away from her."

 Search and Find

2 ants

1 Bible

1 purple scarf

3 brooms

4 bowls

1 red belt

2 butterflies

5 flowers

 3 cups

 **1** blue sash

 Jesus' face

 **1** rug

 7 oranges

 5 jugs

 6 spoons

26
Parable of the Ten Virgins

Matthew 25:1–13

Jesus and His disciples went to the Mount of Olives, where He taught about the end times. "The kingdom of heaven will be like ten virgins who took their lamps and went to meet the bridegroom. Five were wise, and five were foolish. The foolish took their lamps, but no extra oil. The wise took jars of oil along with their lamps. When the bridegroom was late, they became tired and fell asleep. At midnight, someone shouted, 'Look! The bridegroom is coming! Go and meet him!'

"Then all of the virgins got up and started lighting their lamps. The foolish said to the wise, 'Let us have some of your oil; our lamps are going out.'

"'No,' the wise answered, 'there will not be enough for all of us. Go and buy some for yourselves.'

"While they were gone to buy some oil, the bridegroom arrived. Those who were ready went into the marriage feast with him.

"After the doors were closed, the other virgins returned and called out, 'Lord! Lord, open the door for us!'

"'I don't know you,' he answered.

"Watch out," Jesus said, "because you don't know the day or the hour when the Son of Man is returning."

 Search and Find

4 clumps of grass

1 sleeping cat

2 s'mores

3 necklaces

5 crowns

5 lamps not lit

1 moon

4 bracelets

Jesus' face

2 kittens

10 stars

5 lit lamps

1 Bible

27
Triumphal Entry

Luke 19:28–40

When they drew near to Jerusalem and came to the Mount of Olives, then Jesus sent two disciples. He said, "Go into the village in front of you. Immediately, you will find a donkey tied, and a colt with her. No one has ever sat on the colt. Untie them and bring them to Me. If anyone says anything to you, you shall say, 'The Lord needs them.' Then he will send them at once."

The disciples did as Jesus directed them. They found the colt tied at a door outside in the street, and they untied it. The disciples brought the donkey and the colt. They put their cloaks on the animals, and Jesus sat on them.

Most of the crowd spread their cloaks on the road. Others cut branches from the trees and spread them on the road. The crowds that went before Jesus and that followed Him were shouting, "Hosanna to the Son of David! Blessed is He who comes in the name of the Lord! Hosanna in the highest!"

 Search and Find

5 children

7 flowers

1 yellow robe

1 dog bone

1 doll

6 stones

1 Bibl

2 bugs

2 pigeons

2 Roman soldiers

3 dogs

1 man with red hair

Jesus' face

8 palm leaves

28
The Widow's Mite

Luke 19:28–40

Then Jesus sat down near the treasury. He watched the people put money into the offering box. Many rich people put in large sums.

A poor widow came. She put in two small copper coins, which make a penny.

Jesus called His disciples to Him. He said to them, "Truly, I say to you, this poor widow has put in more than all. For they all gave out of their abundance. But she has put in everything she had. It was all she had to live on."

Search and Find

1 recycling bin

4 columns

8 footprints

1 Bible

5 money bags

5 silver coins

8 handprints

Jesus' face

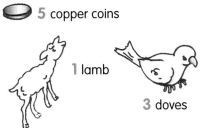
5 copper coins

1 lamb

3 doves

1 offering basket

2 green sashes

1 praying hands

29
Jesus Is Anointed
John 12:1–8

Six days before the Passover, Jesus came to Bethany, where Lazarus lived. Jesus had raised Lazarus from the dead.

They gave a dinner for Jesus there. Martha served, and Lazarus was one of those reclining with Jesus at the table.

Mary took a pound of expensive ointment made from pure nard, and she anointed the feet of Jesus and wiped His feet with her hair.

The house was filled with the fragrance of the perfume.

But Judas Iscariot, one of Jesus' disciples (he was the one who was about to betray Jesus), said, "Why was this ointment not sold for three hundred denarii and the money given to the poor?"

Judas said this not because he cared about the poor but because he was a thief. He was in charge of the moneybag, and he used to help himself to what was put into the bag.

But Jesus said, "Leave her alone, so that she may keep it for the day of my burial. For the poor you always have with you, but you do not always have Me."

Search and Find

3 pillows

2 bowls

3 butterflies

8 hearts

Jesus' face

5 coins

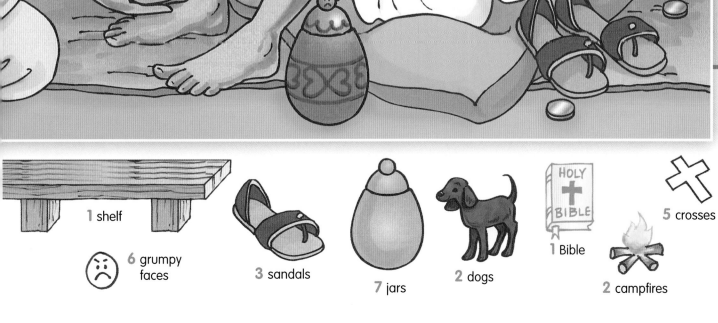

1 shelf

6 grumpy faces

3 sandals

7 jars

2 dogs

1 Bible

5 crosses

2 campfires

30
Jesus Washes Disciples' Feet

John 13:1–17

Jesus and His disciples gathered to celebrate the Passover. Jesus stood up, took off His outer robes, and tied a towel around His waist. Jesus poured water into a basin and began to wash His disciples' feet, drying them with the towel.

When Jesus came to wash Simon Peter's feet; Peter tried to stop Him. But Jesus said, "If I do not wash you, you have no share with Me." Peter did not understand, so he asked Jesus to wash not just his feet, but also his hands and head. Jesus said, "The one who has bathed does not need to wash except for his feet, but is completely clean."

Jesus finished, put his robes back on, and took His place at the table. Jesus said, "Do you understand what I have done to you? You call me Teacher and Lord, and you are right, for so I am. If I then, your Lord and Teacher, have washed your feet, you also ought to wash one another's feet. Truly, truly, I say to you, a servant is not greater than his master, nor is a messenger greater than the one who sent him."

 Search and Find

1 surprised look

 1 pitcher

 6 goblets

 4 flowers

3 pillows

1 blue coat

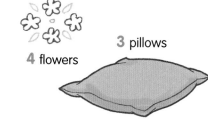

 1 spid[er]

1 Bible

1 man with black hair

Jesus' face

4 bowls

1 red belt

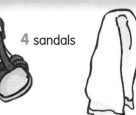
2 butterflies

4 sandals

3 towels

31
Jesus in the Garden
Matthew 26:36–56

Jesus went with the disciples to Gethsemane. Taking with Him Peter and James and John, Jesus said, "My soul is very sorrowful, even to death. Remain here, and watch with Me."

Going a little farther, Jesus prayed. "My Father, if it be possible, let this cup pass from Me. Nevertheless, not as I will, but as You will."

Finding the disciples sleeping, Jesus said, "Could you not watch with Me one hour? Watch and pray that you may not enter into temptation. The spirit indeed is willing, but the flesh is weak."

For the second time, Jesus went away and prayed, "My Father, if this cannot pass unless I drink it, Your will be done."

Again, Jesus found the disciples sleeping. So He went away and prayed for the third time, saying the same words again.

Then Jesus said to the disciples, "The hour is at hand. The Son of Man is betrayed into the hands of sinners. Rise, My betrayer is at hand."

Judas came with a great crowd. He had given them a sign, saying, "The one I will kiss is the man. Seize Him!"

Judas came up to Jesus and said, "Greetings, Rabbi!" And Judas kissed Jesus.

Jesus said, "Friend, do what you came to do." Then they seized Him, and all the disciples left Jesus and fled.

Search and Find

3 nests

10 olives

1 lock

3 clubs

6 bushes

1 cat

3 swords

64

7 rocks

1 blue hat

1 Bible

2 snails

Jesus' face

7 stars

1 red coat

3 torches

32
Jesus Suffers and Dies

Matthew 27:27–54; 28:5–6

Two criminals were led away to be put to death with Jesus. They came to the place that is called The Skull. There they crucified Him and the criminals. One was on His right and one was on His left.

And Jesus said, "Father, forgive them. For they know not what they do."

The people stood by, watching. But the rulers and the soldiers mocked Jesus.

There was darkness over the whole land. Then Jesus called out with a loud voice. He said, "Father, into Your hands I commit My spirit!" And He breathed His last.

A man named Joseph took down Jesus' body. He wrapped it. And he laid Jesus in a tomb cut in stone. The women who had come with Jesus from Galilee followed. They saw the tomb.

On the first day of the week, the women went to the tomb. They found the stone rolled away from the tomb. But when they went in, they did not find the body of the Lord Jesus.

Then, behold, two men stood by them in dazzling apparel. The men said to them, "Why do you seek the living among the dead? Jesus is not here. He has risen!"

Search and Find

3 clouds

10 small crosses

2 plumes

1 helmet

1 sun

1 Bible

2 belts

1 red scarf

Jesus' face

1 first-aid kit

5 rocks

1 crown of thorns

4 birds

3 bushes

33
On the Road to Emmaus

Luke 24:13–35

Two men were going to a village named Emmaus, about seven miles from Jerusalem. As they walked, they talked about Jesus' death and the empty tomb.

While they were walking, Jesus came near. The two men did not know it was Jesus.

Jesus said, "What are you talking about?"

Cleopas said, "Don't You know what things have happened these days?"

Jesus said to them, "What things?"

They said, "Things about Jesus. Our priests and rulers put Him on a cross to die. It is the third day since He died. Some women amazed us. They were at the tomb early this morning. They said they had seen a vision of angels. The angels said Jesus was alive.

Jesus said to them, "But Jesus had to suffer." And He explained the Scriptures about Himself.

When they came near the village, the two men said, "Stay with us. For it is evening. The day is almost over."

When Jesus was at the table, He took the bread and blessed it. Then He broke it and gave it to them. At once, they recognized Him. But He vanished from their sight.

They returned to Jerusalem, found the eleven disciples, and said, "The Lord has risen indeed!"

Search and Find

3 dogs

1 bench

1 walking stick

1 snake

1 oil lamp with a wick

5 jars

7 flowers

1 Bible

7 sheep

1 satchel

6 trees

1 green hat

Jesus' face

1 sun

34
Jesus Ascends to Heaven
Acts 1:9–11

Jesus showed the disciples that He was alive for forty days. He spoke to them about the kingdom of God.

Jesus also told the disciples to stay in Jerusalem. They were to wait there for the promise of the Father. Jesus said, "You will be baptized with the Holy Spirit in a few days."

One day later, Jesus led them to the Mount of Olives. They asked, "Now will You bring back the kingdom to Israel?"

He said, "You do not need to know what God does. You will not know His timing. But you will get power when the Holy Spirit comes to you. You will speak God's Word in Jerusalem. You will be My witnesses to the end of the earth."

As the disciples were looking, Jesus was lifted up. Then a cloud took Him out of sight.

While the disciples were gazing into heaven, Jesus went up. Behold! Two men stood by them in white robes.

The men said, "Men of Galilee, why are you looking into heaven? Jesus was taken up into heaven. He will come back the same way as you saw Him go into heaven."

Search and Find

1 compass

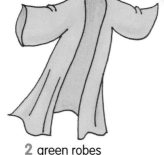
2 green robes

1 Bible

3 spiders

3 clouds

2 angels

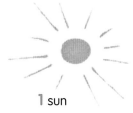
1 sun

5 rocks

Jesus' face

1 mouse

3 butterflies

6 flowers

2 shrubs

35
God Sends the Holy Spirit

Acts 2:1–21, 37–47

On Pentecost, the disciples were together in one place. Suddenly, a sound like a mighty rushing wind filled the entire house. Divided tongues of fire appeared and rested on each of them. They were filled with the Holy Spirit and began to speak in other tongues.

People from every nation in Jerusalem were amazed, saying, "Are not all these Galileans? How is it we hear them telling the mighty works of God in our own language?"

Peter addressed the crowd, "This is what was said through the prophet Joel: 'In the last days I will pour out my Spirit on all flesh. Your sons and daughters shall prophesy, and your young men shall see visions, and your old men shall dream dreams.'"

Peter went on to explain the life and work of Jesus. When the crowd heard this, they were cut to the heart and said, "What shall we do?"

Peter said, "Repent and be baptized every one of you in the name of Jesus Christ for the forgiveness of your sins, and you will receive the gift of the Holy Spirit. The promise is for you and for your children and for all who are far off, everyone whom the Lord our God calls to Himself."

Search and Find

Jesus' face

5 bowls

1 spider

1 striped coat

13 flames

1 green coat

1 Bible

 5 goblets

2 webs

 1 surprised look

1 chair

 1 dove

 1 man with red hair

 2 bracelets

36
Philip and the Ethiopian

Acts 8:26–39

An angel of the Lord said to Philip, "Rise and go toward the south. Take the road that goes from Jerusalem to Gaza." Philip rose and went.

There was an Ethiopian, a court official of Candace, the queen. He had come to Jerusalem to worship. Now he was returning, seated in his chariot, and reading the prophet Isaiah.

The Spirit said to Philip, "Go over and join this chariot."

So Philip ran to him, and heard him reading Isaiah the prophet. Philip asked, "Do you understand what you are reading?"

And he said, "How can I, unless someone guides me?" And he invited Philip to come sit with him.

He was reading, "Like a sheep He was led to death and like a lamb before its shearer is silent, so He opens not His mouth."

The Ethiopian said to Philip, "About whom, does the prophet say this? About himself? About someone else?"

Then Philip, beginning with this Scripture, told him the good news about Jesus.

As they were going along the road they came to some water. The Ethiopian said, "See, here is water! What prevents me from being baptized?" Going down into the water, Philip baptized him.

Search and Find

3 lily pads

1 trail map

4 Baptism shells

3 rings

1 angel

6 dates on palm trees

6 crosses

4 tufts of grass

1 Bible

3 fish

2 frogs

Jesus' face

7 rocks

3 scrolls

37
Peter's Escape from Prison

Acts 12:4–17

Herod the king laid violent hands on some who belonged to the church. He killed James the brother of John. He saw that it pleased the Jews. So he arrested Peter and put him in prison with four squads of soldiers to guard him. The church made earnest prayer for Peter.

That night, Peter was sleeping between two soldiers, bound with chains. Sentries before the door were guarding the prison. And behold, an angel of the Lord stood next to Peter. A light shone in the cell.

The angel struck Peter on the side and woke him. He said, "Get up quickly." And the chains fell off his hands. And the angel said to him, "Dress yourself. Put on your sandals. Wrap your cloak around you and follow me."

So Peter followed him. He thought he was seeing a vision. He did not know that what was being done by the angel was real.

They passed the first and the second guard. They came to the gate leading into the city. It opened for them on its own. They went out and the angel left him.

When Peter came to himself, he said, "Now I am sure that the Lord sent His angel."

Search and Find

1 mouse

1 yellow chain

2 gates

2 praying hands

Jesus' face

1 helmet

1 smiling face

1
red chain

1 Bible

1 sad face

1 moon

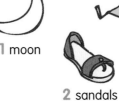
1
blue chain

1 tent

2 sandals

1 cat

1 sleeping face

38
Lydia

Acts 16:11–15

A vision appeared to Paul in the night: a man of Macedonia was standing there. The man urged Paul, saying, "Come over to Macedonia and help us."

When Paul had seen the vision, immediately he planned to go to Macedonia. He believed that God had called him to preach the Gospel there.

So Paul set sail from Troas and arrived in Philippi, which is a leading city of the district of Macedonia and a Roman colony. They remained in this city some days.

On the Sabbath day, the disciples went outside the gate to the riverside, where they supposed there was a place of prayer. They sat down and spoke to the women who had come together.

One of the women who heard them was named Lydia. She was from the city of Thyatira, a seller of purple goods, and she worshiped God. The Lord opened her heart to pay attention to what Paul said. After Lydia was baptized, and her household as well, she urged the disciples, saying, "If you have judged me to be faithful to the Lord, come to my house and stay."

Search and Find

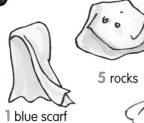
1 blue scarf

5 rocks

2 rabbits

1 water jug

3 butterflies

1 gold bracelet

5 shells

2 nests

1 sail

Jesus' face

1 Bible

1 purple robe

7 cattails

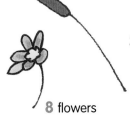
8 flowers

3 praying hands

1 striped coat

6 bushes

39
Paul's Shipwreck

Acts 27:13–44

Soldiers delivered Paul to a Roman centurion named Julius. Julius treated Paul kindly and found a ship sailing to Italy.

Paul said, "I think the voyage will be dangerous for the cargo, for the ship, and for our lives."

Soon there came a dangerous windstorm. The ship was tossed by the storm. The sailors gave up all hope.

Paul said, "Men, I tell you to take heart. An angel of God told me there will be no loss of life. Only the ship will be lost."

When it was day, they saw a bay with a beach. They planned to land the ship there. But the ship hit a reef. The bow stuck. The stern was broken by the waves!

The soldiers planned to kill the prisoners so they could not swim away and escape. But Julius wanted to save Paul. He kept the soldiers from carrying out their plan. He ordered those who could swim to jump overboard first and swim for the land. The rest floated to land on pieces of the ship. They all were brought safely to land.

Search and Find

1 crate

5 birds

7 boards

1 yellow coat

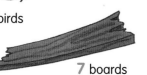

6 rocks

2 barrels

1 Bible

3 turtles

1 man
with red hair

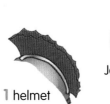
1 helmet

Jesus' face

4 clumps of grass

7 arms

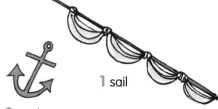
3 anchors

1 sail

40
The River of Life

Revelation 22:1–4

I saw a new heaven and a new earth. The holy city, new Jerusalem, coming down from heaven.

One of the seven angels carried me away in the Spirit to a great, high mountain and showed me the holy city Jerusalem. It had a great, high wall, with twelve gates, and at the gates twelve angels. The names of the twelve tribes of the sons of Israel were inscribed on the gates. The city wall had twelve foundations with the twelve names of the apostles.

I saw no temple in the city, for its temple is the Lord God the Almighty and the Lamb. The city has no need of sun or moon to shine, for the glory of God gives it light. Its lamp is the Lamb. Its gates will never be shut by day—there will be no night.

The angel showed me the river of life, flowing from the throne of God through the middle of the street of the city. On either side of the river was the tree of life. The leaves of the tree were for the healing of the nations. Night will be no more. They will need no light of lamp or sun, for the Lord God will be their light, and they will reign forever and ever.

Search and Find

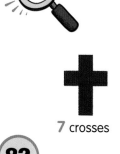

7 crosses

4 gates

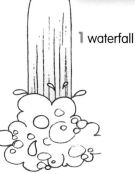

1 waterfall

1 flower

6 trees

Jesus' face

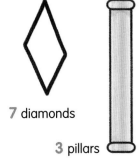
7 diamonds

3 pillars

8 windows

6 purple plums

1 Bible

6 oranges

3 yellow peaches

3 angels

5 red apples

((FAMILY FAITH TALK))

1 Creation page 4

There are many opportunities to marvel at God's creation and talk about His goodness in making the world. Go for a walk together. Use binoculars made with cardboard rolls secured with duct tape to spy God's created things, or take pictures of things you spy as you walk. Print the pictures, and put them in a homemade scrapbook. Thank God for the beautiful world He created. Ask Him to help you be a good caretaker of it.

2 Noah page 6

Take out family Baptism certificates, pictures, and other mementos for each person. Talk about when each of you was baptized—where you were baptized, the words spoken, and who was there. Thank God for rescuing you from sin through Jesus' death on the cross and making you His children through His Word and the waters of Baptism.

3 Tower of Babel page 8

Give each family member a piece of paper. Write your name on your paper and draw a picture of a way God cares for you. Write "God loves you" in a different language on each paper. Tape the papers together into a tower, and talk about your pictures. Thank God for the ways He cares for you, especially for forgiving your sins and giving you eternal life through His Son, Jesus.

4 Birth of Moses page 10

Begin a family journal. Create a basket-weave cover for it. Write on it, "God protects us every day!" Ask family members to tell how God has helped you in times of trouble or illness. Younger children can draw pictures. Record these experiences in your family journal. Thank God for His help and deliverance, especially through Jesus.

5 Passover page 12

Our heavenly Father protects us from all harm and danger. He guards and protects us from all evil. That doesn't mean that nothing bad will ever happen to us. It means God uses His power, wisdom, and strength for our good. When tough situations happen in your family (and they will), look at the situation with eyes of faith. Review with your child how God guided you or brought you through the move, sickness, or trouble. Then pause and thank Him.

6 Crossing the Red Sea page 14

As a family, share times when God has helped you and delivered you from troubles. Write short descriptions about the experiences on a poster or draw pictures of them. Thank God for His deliverance and help. Thank Him for sending Jesus to deliver you from your sins through His death and resurrection.

7 Water from the Rock page 16

As a family, talk about how God cares for you by giving you what you need and works through you to care for others. Decide on a family care project, such as contacting a local food pantry to find out what they need for the people who come. Collect some of the items they need, and as a family, deliver the food to the pantry. If possible, volunteer to help in the pantry on a regular basis.

8 Rahab Believes page 18

List five things you can do to show love for others in your church or community; for example, at a homeless shelter, food pantry, or a home for seniors. Check with the people in charge for when you can visit and additional ways you can help.

((FAMILY FAITH TALK))

9 Hannah's Prayer page 20

Make a family prayer tree. Place a found tree branch in a pot of sand. Trace around your hands onto colorful paper to make leaves shaped like praying hands. Write prayer requests or tape pictures of people or things to pray for on the leaves. Use string to hang them from the branches.

At supper time or bedtime, choose a new leaf and pray for the pictured person or listed prayer request. Talk about how God always hears our prayers for Jesus' sake and will answer in a way that is best.

10 Elijah at the Brook Cherith page 22

Make muffins or other treats to give to others who are lonely or afraid. As you work together, talk about how Elijah may have been scared or lonely when he had to hide from King Ahab, but God was with him. Discuss how God is with you too, no matter what, and also uses you to show love for others and remind them of His love. Take your treats to a lonely neighbor or sick or shut-in person. Spend time visiting and sharing God's love with the person.

11 Elijah and the Widow of Zarephath
page 24

Make a pictorial wreath that reflects how God sustains your family. Take pictures of your home and family, your favorite foods and clothes, and your family at work and play. Attach the photos to the rim of a sturdy paper plate. On the inside of the plate, write these words: "God sustains us by His wisdom and power. He gives us food and clothing, home and family, work and play, and all that we need from day to day." Talk with your children about how God sent Jesus to take care of our greatest need. Jesus is our Savior!

12 Elijah and the Prophets of Baal page 26

God answered Elijah's prayer in a most dramatic way. God hears our prayers and answers them too. Make a prayer chart with one section for things prayed for and another section to show when and how prayers were answered. Have a popcorn prayer, where family members can "pop in" at any point to thank God for His blessings. Conclude by thanking Him for the blessing of Jesus, our Savior.

13 Naaman Healed page 28

God healed Naaman from the disease of leprosy. God heals us too. He heals us when we have physical diseases; He also heals us from the sickness of sin through Jesus' death and resurrection.

Buy or make a first-aid kit. Look at the supplies in the kit and talk about what they are for. Thank God for His healing. Then as a family, decide on a project to help others, such as making health or personal care kits for others. Contact a nursing home or the children's section of a hospital to find out what they need.

14 Isaiah Sees the Lord page 30

Play charades, acting out various professions (e.g., a basketball player, singer, police officer, pastor, or baker). Ask your child or children what they would like to do when they grow up. Help them understand that they can serve others no matter what their life's work turns out to be. And by serving others, they are also serving God.

15 King Josiah page 32

All the words in the Bible are true and tell us of God's love, especially how He sent Jesus to be our Savior. God says His Word always brings about what He wants. Name three places you can hear or read God's Word.

Have family members choose a favorite Bible passage and write it on a piece of paper. Roll up the papers like a scroll. Trade scrolls; then read the verses out loud. Have the person who wrote the verse tell what it means to him or her.

16 Jonah page 34

God forgave Jonah and worked through Jonah to deliver His message to the Ninevites. God forgives you and uses you to share His love with others too.

Draw a big fish outline on poster paper. Inside the fish, write the names of people with whom you can share Jesus' love. Around the fish, write or draw pictures of what you can do to share His love with others. Have family members each choose a name and connect it to something they will do this week for that person so he or she learns about God's love in Jesus.

((FAMILY FAITH TALK))

17 The Birth of Jesus page 36

The Bible tells us that Mary wrapped the human baby Jesus in swaddling cloths and placed Him in a manger. Take a strip of cloth or baby blanket and show your child how to swaddle a baby. Talk about how swaddling helps the baby feel secure. Then remind your child that when Jesus died, He was also wrapped in cloths and placed in the tomb. But Jesus didn't stay in that tomb. He rose from the dead on Easter morning. He didn't need those cloths anymore. His victory secures our salvation.

18 John the Baptist page 38

John proclaimed God's Word. He pointed to Jesus as the Lamb of God, who saves us from our sins. Today, pastors and missionaries tell people about Jesus, the Savior. You can too.

On a piece of paper, draw around your hand with your fingers extended. In each finger, write one truth about Jesus that you can tell others. Thank God for pastors and missionaries who tell about Jesus. Ask God to help you show His love and tell others too.

19 Wedding at Cana page 40

Jesus surprised the bride and groom with the good gift of wine. God surprises us with many good gifts too. The most special gift of all is Jesus, our Savior.

As a family, talk about the good gifts that God gives to each of you. Thank God for His gifts by sharing them with others. Collect some toys, books, and games that are in good shape and donate them to a children's hospital or a homeless shelter.

20 Built on the Rock page 42

Take a family walk and gather some rocks. Have each family member find a large rock. Wash the rocks and then paint them a light color. Use a darker color to paint a cross on each rock. When dry, add a clear coat of shellac. Place the rocks on the table or where you have family devotions to remind you that Jesus is your rock and salvation.

21 Jesus Heals at Bethesda page 44

Reassure your child that Jesus always loves him and can make him well when he is sick or hurt. Jesus uses doctors and nurses as His helpers for people who are sick.

God uses you to show love to the sick too. Make a card or cookies for someone who is sick and deliver it with your child.

22 Jesus Stills the Storm page 46

Just as Jesus' friends the disciples turned to God for help in troubles, lead your children to do the same thing. Sirens sounding? Say a prayer. Hail pounding? Say a prayer. Sickness attacking? Say a prayer. Jesus hears it. He is still at work in the lives of His people. Jesus is the one true God, who came to save us from our sin and promises to be with us always.

23 Jesus and Nicodemus page 48

Jesus explained to Nicodemus that the Holy Spirit works a new birth of faith through Baptism for all who believe. When you talk with your child about Baptism, remind her of the blessings God gives, especially faith to believe in Jesus.

Look through your church directory at the pictures of all the people who are part of God's family. Have your child talk to her godparents and thank them for praying for her spiritual growth.

24 Good Samaritan page 50

Everyone is our neighbor, especially those who need help. Draw a big heart and decorate it. Write the names of people you know who need help inside the heart. Brainstorm ways to show God's love for them. Have each family member choose a person from the heart, a way to help him or her, and a day this week to carry out the loving action.

((FAMILY FAITH TALK))

25 Mary and Martha page 52

Make edible Bibles by using frosting to decorate graham wafers to look like Bibles. Talk about how food satisfies physical hunger for a while, but then we are hungry again. How does God's Word satisfy us in a different way? Brainstorm ways that you can "hear, read, mark, learn, and inwardly digest" God's Word. Discuss why that is important.

26 Parable of the Ten Virgins page 54

Although parables are hard for young children to understand, you can help teach the point: Jesus gives us faith and makes us ready for the time when He comes to take us home to be with Him. While we wait, we seek to hear God's Word and use His Sacraments. We want Jesus to keep our faith strong.

What can you do to be ready? Regularly go to church and Sunday School. Speak confidently and with joy about how Jesus makes you ready to be with Him. Treasure His Word and read it together.

27 Triumphal Entry page 56

Make a praise banner to hang in your home. Use green markers or crayons to draw a large palm leaf on a piece of poster board. Add the words "Hosanna! Christ is our King" to the poster. Add happy faces. Sing a favorite song to praise Jesus and wave your banners.

28 The Widow's Mite page 58

The Holy Spirit moved a poor woman of God to give a rich offering—all she had. As you prepare your offerings for church and Sunday School, invite your child to be part of that experience. Share with him or her the joy you have in giving. Together, recognize this as the work of the Holy Spirit, who gives us faith and helps us give others the gifts God has given to us.

29 Jesus Is Anointed page 60

The Holy Spirit works in the lives of God's children. The Holy Spirit creates in God's children a selfless and generous love. The woman in the Bible story was criticized for showing that kind of love.

When you see this selfless love in your child, thank God. His Spirit is at work, helping your child say no to sin and yes to living as God's child. This Spirit-filled living includes praying, going to church, resisting temptations, and saying "I am sorry" and "I forgive you."

Draw around your child's hands onto poster paper. Inside the hands, have your child write or draw ways he or she can show love this week. Then pray for God the Holy Spirit's help in doing this.

30 Jesus Washes Disciples' Feet page 62

Make a service coupon book. Discuss ways members of your family can serve one another. Write or draw pictures of the ideas on note cards. Put the cards in a recipe box. Each night this week, have each person in the family choose a card and then do what it says. Put the used cards back in the back of the box so they will cycle to the front again. Ask God to help you serve one another with gladness.

31 Jesus in the Garden page 64

Write the letters of the alphabet in a vertical row on a piece of paper. Look at a globe or world atlas, and find countries that begin with each letter. Write the names beside the letters.

Then begin with the letter *A* and pray for the people in the country that they may learn about Jesus' love and forgiveness. The next night, pray for the people in the country that starts with a *B,* and so forth.

32 Jesus Suffers and Dies page 66

On the cross, Jesus paid for our sins and rose again on Easter. Go on a hunt for crosses. When you find one, show your child how to take a digital picture of the cross. What kinds of crosses did you find? Let the crosses remind you and your child that Jesus is our Savior from sin, death, and the devil.

((FAMILY FAITH TALK))

33 On the Road to Emmaus page 68

Have family members draw around their shoe, cut out the footprint shape, and decorate it. On each footprint, write the name of someone you can invite to church to hear about Jesus and how He died and rose again to pay for our sins.

Put the footprints in a bag, shake it up, and select a footprint. Invite the person named on the footprint to church this week. Offer to pick the person up, and consider inviting him or her to dinner after church.

34 Jesus Ascends to Heaven page 70

Jesus ascended into heaven to prepare a place for us. Jesus ascended to the right hand of the Father, but He is also with you to the very end of time.

Set ten objects on a table. Have your child close his or her eyes while you remove an object. Then have your child guess the object you took. After your child guesses, return the object that was hidden from view. Take turns hiding objects and naming what's missing. Remind your child that even though we don't see Jesus now, He promises to return.

35 God Sends the Holy Spirit page 72

Pentecost is the birthday of the Christian Church. Make and decorate cupcakes to celebrate. Put candles on each cupcake and light them. Observe the flames, and talk about how the tongues of fire at Pentecost were a sign of the Holy Spirit's empowering presence.

36 Philip and the Ethiopian page 74

God had an angel send Philip to help a man from Africa who did not understand the words Isaiah the prophet wrote about Jesus. Many people do not understand God's Word. You can support the work of our local church as it spreads the Gospel through offerings and prayer. You might also consider donating a children's Bible in honor of your child to your local library so other children may come to believe in Jesus as their Savior and be in His family.

37 Peter's Escape from Prison page 76

As you put your children to sleep at night, remind them with words, pictures, and prayers that God's holy angels watch over them. Tell them God's angels are many and powerful. Clarify any misunderstandings about angels, such as the belief that angels are people who have died and gone to heaven.

38 Lydia page 78

Through Baptism, God makes you part of His family. Look at your church directory. These are brothers and sisters in Christ. Draw the outline of a church on a piece of paper. Write the names of those on your church prayer list inside the shape. Pray for them.

39 Paul's Shipwreck page 80

Make a list of people God uses to protect your family. These could include firefighters, police officers, soldiers on your church's prayer list, parents, teachers, or crossing guards. Send a card to someone on your list to thank the person for protecting your family. Thank God for these people too!

40 The River of Life page 82

Revelation says there will be no more tears or sadness in heaven. All things will be new, and we will see Jesus face-to-face. As a family, draw a large mural of what you think heaven will be like. Who are some people you want to see in heaven? What will you talk about? What will you do there?